IMMUNE TO THE SACRED

OTHER BOOKS BY THE AUTHOR

All of Us, Reticent, Here, Together (Mansfield Press, 2016)
Where Did You See It Last? (Textualis Press, 2016)
Images from Declassified Nuclear Test Films (above/ground press, 2014)
Complete Surprising Fragments of Improbable Books (Mansfield Press, 2013)
Excerpts from Improbable Books, The Apt. 9 Installment (Apt. 9 Press, 2013)
Excerpts from Impossible Books, The Crawdad Cantos (above/ground press, 2012)
Rogue Stimulus: The Stephen Harper Holiday Anthology for a Prorogued Parliament, (co-editor, Mansfield Press, 2011)
Impossible Books, The Carleton Installment (above/ground press, 2010)
From Impossible Books (Olive Reading Series, 2007)
The Real Made Up (ECW Press, 2007)
O Helios (Olive Reading Series, 2005)
Fruitfly Geographic (ECW Press, 2004)
Cometology (ECW Press, 2001)
Marin County Poems (above/ground press, 2001)
The Wire in Fences (Balmuir Poetry Series, 1988)

IMMUNE TO THE SACRED

STEPHEN BROCKWELL

Mansfield Press

Printed in Canada

Library and Archives Canada Cataloguing in Publication

Title: Immune to the sacred / Stephen Brockwell.
Names: Brockwell, Stephen, author.
Description: Poems.
Identifiers: Canadiana 20220226032 | ISBN 9781771262811 (softcover)
Classification: LCC PS8553.R6135 I46 202 | DDC C811/.54—dc23

Typesetting and design: Denis De Klerck
Cover Art: Ingrid Dabringer
Author Photo: Kira Harris

The publication of *Immune to the Sacred* has been generously supported by the Canada Council for the Arts and the Ontario Arts Council.

ONTARIO ARTS COUNCIL
CONSEIL DES ARTS DE L'ONTARIO
an Ontario government agency
un organisme du gouvernement de l'Ontario

Canada Council for the Arts
Conseil des arts du Canada

Mansfield Press Inc.
25 Mansfield Avenue, Toronto, Ontario, Canada M6J 2A9
Publisher: Denis De Klerck
www.mansfieldpress.net

For Michael Dennis

CONTENTS

The moment you say that any idea system is sacred, whether it's a religious belief system or a secular ideology, the moment you declare a set of ideas to be immune from criticism, satire, derision, or contempt, freedom of thought becomes impossible.

—Salman Rushdie

FLEE THE CELESTIAL GLITTERING OF TWILIGHT PHUKET SKYSCAPES

There are nights the krill
phosphoresce when you drag your hand
beside the kayak
under a new moon.

It's like casting a spell
that transmutes
silt into platinum,
a spiny lobster into
a resident surgeon.

Look at your hand. Gaze upon
your very hand—
its palm and fingers:

a starfish
on the starfish of your body.

You. You are
transformed!

SAINT PATRICK

I'm walking toward the Rideau River
past the razor-wire-topped cinder-block walls
of the nineteenth-century monastery
Notre-Dame de Charité du Refuge
that's hosted the Chinese embassy for years.
Little-known fact: the chapel spire was torn down;
in a photo from the sixties the tin
flèche and cross gleam in the winter sunlight.
I wonder what happened to the chalice.
Across the street, a patient Falun Gong
protester encamps on a tarp in the grass
in Sukhasana pose. Behind her,
a placard of disappeared believers
curls. A Cadillac Escalade honks.
My daughter studied photography
at De La Salle high school on the south side
of St. Patrick Street. Students chase after
a soccer ball that pings off the school fence.
I am reading a poem by a poet
I'd like to forget. He writes about
his infant daughter's delicate body
on a sheepskin rug in the living room.
She is a turtle encircled by crows,
the faces of the men in her future.
I hear the flying oil slick of a crow
land on a lamppost and *caw*! A living
gargoyle announces the apocalypse.
I'm tempted to caw back but there are clouds,
cars passing, children playing, a woman
meditating on her lost fellowship
with the disappeared. I take a photo
of the crow with the poem in my hand, tweak
depth of field to capture crow and page,
focus sharply enough to read the text.

Intersecting fields of view expand; my eyes
assemble memories as real as the event.
I won't recall a thing after the crow
flies over the embassy and river
to a road with higher carrion yields.
I won't remember walking home.
Stay with me, Saint Patrick. Help me to wait
long enough in wet grass to take this in.
Let your ash walking stick take root here.
Teach me to love without violence.

WHY YOU CAN'T HAVE BEAUTIFUL THINGS

Here is a beautiful thing: a cuttlefish tattoos itself the mottle
sepia of the reef.

Here is a beautiful thing: the tardigrade clambers up a
ladder of algae.

Here is a beautiful thing: a wasp heavy with nectar harvests
one last purple crocus.

Here is a beautiful thing: the invisible diatom's shell,
architectural glass assembled from dissolved silicon.

Here is a beautiful thing: a black squirrel puffs out its grey
winter undercoat.

Here is a beautiful thing: the gait of a cockroach escaping an
incandescent bulb.

Here is a beautiful thing: you! Look at your hands—they are
capable of so much, even nothing!

Here was a beautiful thing: the pangolin.

Here was a beautiful thing: the red wolf.

Here was a beautiful thing: the bumblebee.

Here was a beautiful thing: you.

STILL FROM DECLASSIFIED NUCLEAR TEST FILM: LET'S FACE IT

Her hair.
Say that—all the voices
murmur.

Skin tone
adjustments I can't
imagine—who could?
No categories for that
declassification, too much
gamma
to see it.

And of the trees,
what survives?
Matchsticks can't make
survival
as beautiful as a sunset.

There are no creams
for alpha particles.

0800055, Undated, 9:35–10:04

CONVOCATION ADDRESS

To find new ways to say nothing of importance
is half the art of poetry, never mind the sweat.
Who among you passed finals by answering
half the questions perfectly, begging part marks
from clever guesses, hoping to squeeze
enough to lift you to that long-sought degree?
Show of hands! The TA of Computational
Politics held you in their red Bic pen.
Let's examine the examiner for a sec.
Question 4:
Prove the human heart has no material
necessity for the expression of love.
Question 4a:
Use the cultural calculus of personhood
to map the nexus of that metaphor,
heart. At some point, a lurching
zombie in a leotard is no longer a theatrical
proposition. A mummy in a tomb has a heart
intact, a brain yanked out the nostrils,
garbage. Who needs ventilating lobes
in a stone bed in the desert?
Keep a lid on that password to the halls
of Eleusis. No decryption; no entry. Access
denied to the crypt where lie the cremains
of a mountain of small lies
one yodel from a catastrophic avalanche
no subsnowcrustian meadow vole has ever
detected with its sensitive epithelial cells.
It elides the pine tops and their nesting
raptors. A mountain hare, ears back, is astonished
to see such egg on the face of the escarpment.
Let's cleave unto the inalienable
truth trumpeted through a megaphone
at the summit of Mount Indifference:

the heart pumps blood until the blood it pumps
stalls in the plaque of an artery
that feeds blood to the heart.
"Well," answers the hematologist,
"kidney, pancreas, spleen, marrow,
platelet, erythrocyte, leukocyte, plasma."
The neurologist exits the elevator
blinking. Full stop. Soul evacuates
to a swaying pine top for a last
glance at a snowflake melting
on a toddler's tongue.
You recognize that toddler. Your heart
thup-a-thup-a-thups as steadily
as a quasar's cosmic radiance.
Thup-a, thup-a, thup-a, thup-a.
You love the little mirror in the snow.

SAN BERNARDINO FREEWAY, VERY LATE

Twist your face, ape.
Shuffle on the green
as a gibbon in a jungle garden

trapezes canopy branches,
then perambulates the forest floor,
arms up, "Who, me?"

Your numberless consorts
cling to the cash in the pockets
of your cashmere overcoat.

The gibbon, monogamous,
eloquent, sings
amorous oratorios

and lamentations of the leopard
skulking under the fig tree.
O great ennobled gibbon!

You slur, cart-driven cur. Spurned
shambolic goblin, wielding sand
wedge and blood cap, your clan

of suite-caged hairless primates
are paragons of the grasping caste.
Hucksters under your plane tree.

As honest as a drop
of acid rain,
you ape a species of extinct man.

Homo minimanus, cross your arms and frown.
You're expelled from the profession of the clown.

INCOMPLETE UNDERSTANDING OF CLOUDS

If you think the clouds are water
it's been too long since you
sprawled on the summer grass

and called to them, as you watched
seagulls fly under their beards—
or sun-cloud skirts if you prefer.

The clouds thicken in abundant
heat the planet holds to its savannahs
at your insistence.

Sedge and bulrushes remain
a wild and hairy green of meadows.

Clouds were never water for you
but steam: work waiting for a turbine to spin.
There is no water in that lake.

Electrons wait there to illuminate
the boundaries of your breath

when you walk home on winter evenings,
to brighten midnight and obscure
the horizon's belt of anonymous stars.

SCHRÖDINGER PSALM

O bosons, fermions, and quantum fields
that brought into being this habitable world
by chance—help me understand the loaded die
of high finance our landlords cooked up
by design to cheat your inexorable chaos.
Those who turn improbability into profit thrive.
Help me thrive. Deal me an ace after this jack-
shit so I can pay my taxes and my daughter's tuition.
Lock our cats out of Schrödinger's box in a single state
of purring ecstasy so their fur may comfort me
when my daily coin toss lands spinning on its edge.
Give these felines, incapable of evil,
independent trials of mercy at your craps table
of chaotic cellular division. Let me suffer for them.

THE HITCHHIKER'S GUIDE TO BORDER CROSSINGS

1

Phil, we remarked on your broad lapels.
You were thumb-wheeling home to your brother's funeral
in a vintage three-piece you bought on the Main—
black wool with satin piping, better suited to a prom.
It had seen more years than you, more than your brother.
So we drove you to Niagara Falls
and there you crossed over.

2

Jasmine, you carried two babies—
one in your arms—fleeing the fists
of your first beau, Jean-Paul. Infant and backpack.
Goth makeup stayed put in the rain.
Your accidental son a shield against creeps.
We drove you to Cornwall Island
and there you crossed over.

3

Kelly and Steve, bounced out the side door
at the Maples, it wasn't my habit to shepherd
intoxicated souls, but your adolescent faces
recalled that dealer in the back seat of a Charger who
pushed my face toward the pavement at a hundred klicks.
So, I drove you to Coteau-du-Lac.
From there you crossed over.

4

What were your names, pair of young musicians
playing Wilco, Dar Williams, and Uncle Tupelo
until you fell asleep with one hour left in the ride
to Napanee? You had a Buffalo gig.
It seemed aspirational. Maybe you never gave your names.
A parent drove you to Alexandria Bay
where you crossed over.

5

Samir, we pleaded with you not to go, but you
were a Pierrefonds jock with a cross on your neck
and a duffle bag of gear on your pallet-wide shoulders.
No missed Greyhound could hold your superb hands back
from that football camp in Syracuse.
We drove you to Prescott.
We heard you didn't cross.

6

Who was the driver, Seidu Mohammed, who called 911
after you walked seven hours through waist-deep snow,
after a $400 cab ride in North Dakota,
hoping to share an intimate life under the rainbow flag,
not behind bars? You lost your fingers to the frost.
You walked to Manitoba
and you crossed.

FRIGATEBIRD

To be shat upon from the stratosphere
is no small miracle of gravity
and trade winds. But to be shoulder-splattered
by a carob-centred white dot, an eye
of soaring seabird stool, is to be granted
the voice of a bard to tap the Saxon
spring for expletives. Frank Ebanks tells me
the frigatebird is no Canada goose;
it plies the up-and-down drafts with the grace
of Martha Graham in a gossamer dance—
breathtaking. But it's air-bound; one wet feather
and say goodbye to soaring with the clouds.
An exercise in breeding: the frigate class
won't get their feathers wet. If they did,
they might never breed or feed the brood
left on shore. One takes the privilege
of effortless flight to an extreme, cleans
its feathers, preens. He hangs out with the clouds
as a 10 million dollar southpaw,
driving his Tesla to the mound, opens
the gull-wing doors to throw a slider,
nicks the strike box at the bottom left
while polishing his alligator wallet.
Such effortless excellence is a joke.
If geese waddle along the muddy shore,
wade near riverbanks to feed on cattails
and snails in the algae-plagued reeds,
they make a waypoint of cattle corn fields
to graze abandoned cobs, and, when they fly,
they shit on us with artless abundance.

WE ALL HAVE WANTS

I want ice cream.
You want to scream.
All the fallen angels
fly around the house
and board up the casement windows.

They want fine wine.
You offer brandy and cider.
And all the fallen angels
hammer the boards
with fists the size of Toronto.

The dog in his bed covers his head
with shaggy fashion wallets for paws.
And all the fallen angels
adore him, praise him, and sigh
as trumpets would sigh if they could.

You crawl up to bed, cover your ears.
I crank the volume on repeats of *Cheers*.
And all the fallen angels
eat ripe damson plums
and watch Ted Danson wash glasses.

AURORAS, BORIS, ALICE

They remembered the night
auroras trimmed the summer sky

with green and golden hat
ribbons the way milliners do

when they make hats—
not for the young

who buy lids after all—
but for the forsaken

for whom much saké
has been poured and into whom

many tears have been eye-dropped—
so much rice!

NO SOLICITING

I draped the carcass of an American
eel over the gate of the white picket fence

that opens onto my property
and the marble paving stones

no one in my neighbourhood
can afford. My next-door neighbour

William—don't call him Bill—tells me
not even the postman will open my gate

with that eel lock until some raven
hauls it to the park and feeds on it,

beak open, threatening even me,
at which point, I guess, I'll go fishing.

The postman darkens my door
with bills and flyers, nothing

that pleases me. There are things,
coquettish, lush.

No ice cream on this planet
is as delicious as privacy.

STILL FROM DECLASSIFIED NUCLEAR TEST FILM: OPERATION PLUMBBOB

It was a soap bubble
from a plastic garden loop
between the camera
and the sun.

Remember the day.
She was eleven. All of eleven.
Suffering behind her, and ahead.

Grass, yes,
but the emulsion didn't
catch it.

Joy and dish gloves—
merciful lemon cake,

candle enough for
every when and everyone
in the wind of its matter.

0800022-0800022, May 28–October 7, 1957

SOUTHERN DESERT WIND

A desert wind cools you down if you sip
enough water and wear a broad-brimmed hat.
A litre every hour hydrates you
enough to find a succulent to fold
into your senses, to smell its sweet nectar,
watch the sun energize its green stems
and make it bloom. You touch a cactus spine
and bleed in the sand to mark your presence.
You watch a pebble-sized beetle get stuck
on that drop of blood. Bet it takes a sip
before the blood clots; you would too if you
dwelled here. Inhale the perfume of the scrub.
But don't walk too far out on the salt flat.
Don't become prosciutto for coyotes.

TOOTHLESS VIPER

By my age my father had lost mouthfuls of teeth:
two sets organically raised from his gums,
replacements cast in vulcanite, moulded from plastic.
One good year, he could afford a porcelain set.
They gave him the smile of a star.
All disposed outside his body:
dumped in a landfill, incinerated, lost at sea.
At least one set had a waypoint at a no-tell motel.
I recall he came home once without them
at midnight and slid in spares.
The Caribbean Sea extracted
the rogue's porcelain set with a rogue wave.
Now they rest under beach sand,
buried for future archaeologists
to discover when they dig up our era
with tools of new alloys—or, maybe, stone.
A last pair sat bedside in a glass of distilled water.

I've owned two sets of teeth, both biological.
The milk teeth twins of my fingers and toes,
exchanged by fairies for quarters, settle in a landfill
north of Montreal, at least some dentin intact
that identify me as my father's child.
Four were incinerated in my university days.
An aging Russian dentist with poplar trunk arms
yanked them with pliers and local anaesthetic.
In bright pink scrubs she taught me to accommodate
a medicated death. I was left with February nights of teeth
tucked in the soft sockets of my dental alveoli,
fed, bathed, talked over, ground down, given thanks.

CATHEDRAL

It was time to
zero in on
the cathedral,

to reckon the square
it took possession of,
to observe

the moon above the bell tower—
not full, waxing,
near apogee,

but bright enough
to cast shadows
with sharper edges

than the street light
at the corner.

It was time to attend
to the voices there,
to focus the ears

on what must have been
a Latin hymn.
I'm reluctant to speak of it;

I'm part
of a dubious crowd,
rolling my eyes

at the mere suggestion—
watching the woman
pray. It was an interval,

a sustained fourth from a choir
that made me
consider the proposition:

the experience of a relic is not
archaeological.

MIRACLES OF THE SACRED REPLACEMENTS

Look, my terrier puppy bears wings.
Each morning, my tabby sings arias for kibble.
My painted turtle dances for jars of flies.
My opossum shreds lettuce with a saw.
Jane's ferret bathes itself with a loofah!
My brindled hound fetches apples for pies.
See the squirrel on that man's hat?
Good fortune and long life will follow him.
Watch our German shepherd wrestle clowns.
Our marmoset has burrowed a nest in our mattress.
The emu saved us from the burglar. Poor burglar.
My elected representatives perform for treats;
they vote by wagging primate hands
and bray, "Yea" and "Nay."

STILL FROM DECLASSIFIED NUCLEAR TEST FILM: STARFISH PRIME

Burning birch—
that shape,
canopy of fire.

Sap smoke.
Anchor of the trunk
more membrane of flame
than memory of
wood, water.

More energy
in that burn
north of Témiscamingue

than in this megaton,
framed.

0800062, 1962

SOUTH FLORIDA VACATION

1

You gather scattered shells
left behind
near running

barefoot children,
medical bracelets
engraved,

glimmering too.
Shells gleam
in the sand,

gravel, sea spray,
sunlight.

2

The children touch

blood, ash.
Sulphur lingers in the atom-sphere.
Out of the shell,

slugs
make their way through
human tracts,

hasty, eviscerating.
The water-borne
roots of the mangroves

harbour delicate mycelium.

CEILING

1

For corporate folk with experience
it was like a call on a bond that had maxed,
or, for yokels who aren't familiar with such parlance,
a doghouse ceiling for the dog that won't hunt,

or, maybe, the inside top of a can of beans
that a living thing briefly tried to leave.
Everyone implied that the cobwebs
were the peak of her career, that she'd have to climb

the ladder—with her limbs, they said—to reach
that plateau (or the surface underneath,
which is the nature of a ceiling, after all).
The dust there was noticed by all.

"Doesn't dust always fall?" a junior asked.
One of us clarified, authoritatively,
"Electrostatic charge, minimal but sufficient,"
to the partners' nods and shrugs.

2

I remember painting my mother's farmhouse
kitchen ceiling with primer and oil-based white enamel
for what seemed like years—we thought we'd
crouch under countless layers of paint

before we could declare, with certainty,
"No trace of nicotine there." Upside of that labour:
we'd dropped the ceiling for future visitors;
downside, the ceiling paint was always tacky.

When I was a younger man, handiwork was my—
jam, I think you call it. For all the glass ceilings
my mother cut a hole through with inherited glazier skills,
her uncut-diamond way of the tongue,

she made us drop that farmhouse ceiling
we should have painted an accommodating colour.
Jesus, we should have taken the kitchen down to studs.
No, we should have burned the house to ash.

EPISTEMODOGGY

My dog has learned
to remove
winter booties.
He can't
put them on.

Gabriel,
from my wardrobe
of suits, long underwear,
threadbare socks
and self-delusion,

teach me to wear
the transparent
sweater
my mother knit,
the one with
too many arms.

Teach me the trick
of putting on more
than airs. Feed me
a slice of liver.
Make me sit.

LASER SCANNING PSALM

I've been trying to measure the elevation of the sky,
eyeballing the distance to the prairie
from a coach seat on a 737
and spitballing the bottom of that anvil
from my gazebo rocking chair.
About the height of this beer-froth atmosphere
that keeps the birds and UAVs aloft, I know nada.
Engineers of earth and sky, custodians
of cantilevered bridge and geodesic dome—
unpack your laser scanners from their aluminum crates.
Measure the sagging gut of the lowest cloud.
Scan the altitude of the highest-ascending, smallest
red pill of ionospheric hydrogen. Tell me,
before I drink myself to death, if the sky is falling.

PORTRAIT OF THE POET IN THREE CONCUSSIONS

Blaaam! January 1971.

They were upset. Tripped
by skates that were
no longer
under his feet, thanks to
Lesley Leslie's scarf yank.

Wanker! Coat was black.
Duffle buttons
little fat man atom bombs.
What they would have given
to have had his fingers on a button
and breakfall ninja-style.

They could have been some body,
a cerebral child celebrity
in a class of twenty, agile, sick,
holding court. Glowing.
Broken head instead.

How pleasant it could have been,
eschewing the vomit of untreatment,
dodging its necessity
with feline reflexes and charm.
On the rink-dozer front, all quiet. Good lad.
No screens to exacerbate his eyes.

How did they carry him forth
to the couch in the principal's office?
Hero or stoat? Hoisted or hauled?
Did his blades drag on the snow,
his first illegible scrawl?

Dr. Bradford intoned, "Diffuse axonal
injury and celery obfuscation
of cog notion, do not to worry."
Details of the neurological
short-circuit short story
escaped him like the tomcat in the backyard
hauling its scarlet cardinal home.

Kapow! September 1981.

Coach rant on the pigskin
scrubland, mud flat.
"You oddly coddled
mallard egg,
mandrake
root monkey."

Yolk's on you, coach!
Well, on your shirt,
florid as forgotten summer days.
"Mind your manners,
middlin' mustard skein!"
Enough with your paunchy sauces
and patriarchal sausage fillers.
Monday is all offal, no wheat.
Stuff the whole organ
in its church-of-the-evaporated-soul,
organically sourced stomach casing.

At the back of your monde
a deformed sphere of distress,
antebellum cerebellum,
off-balance. A helmet
must always intimately wrap

the head.
Swaddle it. Cradle
with mama bear zeal.
The helmet gives birth after the whistle,
a fractured caesarean
of tender eyes, lobes.

What orbits these daze
but a contusion of worldly
matters and heady regrets
that seem a projection
of your and His disorder,
ineternal distress, your disinclination
to ruminate on more than cud.

Watch the sunlight catch
the satellite of your delusions
on its re-entry. On the horizon
it burns on by.

Krakk! Summer 1991.

No catalogue of my raiding
of the neutron
and the—whatchamacallit—
dent-rite: the sin apes
and their violent scribbles
ion the tree sand.

It will all be sand. Patients.
Skittish pug, your curls
alarm me all morning
with their tesla coils. I'm shocked.
No more bleating!
Bream me up, little brine flesh
in a sea flood of see blood.

All season with your suffering
microplasmotic gillspasms.
See references in appendix.
Over there, in stainless steel
kidney-shaped organelle receptacle 5-A—
the little grey matter
resembling obsolete
abominable gizzard.

Thank you, Doctor.
All treatments welcome;
incisor diagnosis there.
Unwrap it. Dose me.

If ever I had a mandate,
that calendar is obsolete.
Julian, so long. Mayan, goodbye.
Gregorian chant
of mansplaining cant,
I'm spent.

My skin
bronzes in the grass.
Seed time in the autumn breeze.
Tick, tick. Not time passing
but Lyme vectors scalp-rooting
in the planet's timeless communion.

I BECOME A MIGRATORY ANIMAL

I'd walk across the country in a year
if I could step out the front door. I'd call
home from Banff, my voice simultaneous

with you. But if the sun were to dispatch
a signal with its light, "I love you, dear,"
I'd miss the moment, eight minutes late

for that departed train of illumination.
Vega, when you glittered on the western
horizon, who did you shine for? I'll walk

to their grave and share your message.
Vega, what can I do with your weightless light
but end this correspondence here and go?

STILL FROM DECLASSIFIED NUCLEAR TEST FILM: OPERATION SANDSTONE

Dramatic introductory music.

Had to print it out,
enlarge it,
balance
colour.

Light table.
Reading glasses.
OED microfont glass.

Those pixels
must have been a man,
or an animal
prior to the fireball,
the shockwave—

or was it an artifact
of the image,
reproductive noise?

0800003–0800005, Blast Measurement Group

LIGHT TABLE PSALM

"Smite absolutely everyone, Lord,"
beg we who snack at Your light table
of life events, littering muffin crumbs
on Sandra's birthday, staining Albert's heart
attack with coffee rings, bringing no mercy.
For nobody vectors iniquity
like zealous, anthropoid us, Lord. Like us
in outrage—puffed-up, salivating, loud,
wronged by the exotic, shaded other, us.
Lord, those in the know have never seen
a finger of Yours smite a mite or mother.
You gaze at the negatives through a loupe,
weeping from one lens onto another,
blurring the image of our self-destruction.

SHOWERING AFTER A LONG FLIGHT

The scent of sweat entices you,
intimate partner. I offer my pores

to you—your abdomen engorges,
darkens. A drop of water

ten times your mass
affixes your wings to travertine.

A thread of my blood drains from you:
illegible graffiti.

SUNKEN MONUMENTS

Soon everything will happen above ground,
in the ocean that covers everything—
a fluid inner space seething with predators.

Maybe raptors will adapt to this liquid world,
and sea and air will be places of safety
for the highest flyers and their webbed talons.

A man in a boat smokes the last cured leaf
of Virginia tobacco, chugs the last bottle of Coors,
views the last drops of a woman's blood on broken glass

on the sodden deck, the last silk threads
ripped from mannequin hips. This last man
will scream denials so loudly you—

a future you, neither man nor woman, nor
human—will hear his cries over waves,
echoing around the planet, breaking laws

of physics with prep-school fists, grinding
the kind of jaw Gutzon Borglum designed
Mount Rushmore to enpetrify. Imagine

that white granite face hewn into an eternity
of tangs and damselfish that feast
on the coral polyps of rock-face lips.

I should clarify. It was not a man on a boat.
In a boat, it was a photograph of a man
screaming. The loudest photograph ever snapped.

A FEW TOO MANY PARASOLS FOR ME

The shoreline will recede
in the distant future—
let's pick an incongruous temporal analogy
to motivate your misperception of time,
let's intimate that the future
can be counted in sleeps, or moonrises,
that tomorrow is as distant as next year; after all,
next year's tomorrow is also Tuesday and what
will really change? If we were there to witness
the water crawl back under the rock,
the sand climb out of the water,
the reefs pull themselves from the breakers
as a human swimmer, so many—
pick your time interval—
as a human swimmer seconds ago
pulled her muscled shoulders
out of the water from the deep end of the pool
after two dozen freestyle laps—if the reefs
were to rise so from the surf with fish
corpses, bleached coral, crustacean
exoskeletons, not one of them
flapping, pale calcium ghosts
with broad white smiles in fleshless gills,
one blue lobster twenty yards out—no,
hang on, that's a blue vinyl rainboot.
My vision degrades with each
witnessing, with each bead—manufactured
not by friction with its siblings in the surf,
but by a factory southwest of the Yangtze—each bead
and each length of nylon twine in the bowel of a sea
resident. The smoke from wildfires casts a pall over this
rum-soaked tropical fantasy.
Stiffening lenses are the least of my worries.

STILL FROM DECLASSIFIED NUCLEAR TEST FILM: OPERATION TEAPOT (I)

So many objectives:

desert flowers,
mountain sunset,
cup and horizon
at the moment
of creation.

Intimate art
of dust, sand
made glass,
heart lens

of the perishable
mood, desire,
its pitch and yaw,
an orientation

flexible, but its progeny
vivid, immediate,
blood-stopping.

0800017, February 18–May 15, 1955

HARRIET'S FUNERAL

The old man wept
and said Harriet's death
was unfathomable.
Half a dozen parishioners
reached for
their phones. Their small
aluminum yokes.

The old man's eulogy
held other antique phrases but who
heard them over
the grandparents'
keening?

The discomfort of feeling
nothing
was mitigated by the
sandwiches the Auxiliary
prepared for the wake.

Hushed conversations
about the difference
between sympathy
and empathy.

I tried to open
my open eyes
but all of us
remained in the same
chapel at the same time.

Harriet's doppelgänger
was pale and motionless.
Where was Harriet?

SAD CHILD, HAPPY CHILD

An unhappy child in an unhappy world,
the world hugged you
like a mama anaconda.
You spat in its eyes
and wailed.

An unhappy child in a happy world,
you pissed on your privilege,
a drunk on a sacred monument.
The flowers wilted at night;
weeds sprouted in the morning.

A happy child in a happy world,
you loved encyclopedias!
The sparrows chirped
beautiful sad songs.
You drew them with crayons for praise.

A happy child in an unhappy world,
you logged an old forest
to clear a small plot
for your cottage. The flames
were a beautiful sight,
the stumps a fine source of fuel.

BIRD FEEDING

Attempted hurdle of a barbed
wire fence in Bermuda
shorts—
leap of hubris.

Sunset merges
the gold of hay stub,
oat straw,
shrub, wire.

Barb-marked on
the knee, the red
seconds
of a scar's birth.

A tiny filet
of human flesh
for the stomach
of a twittering shrike.

STILL FROM DECLASSIFIED NUCLEAR TEST FILM: TONOPAH TEST RANGE

The bird @ 9:17

The thought was
everything
could be delivered by cannon—

The point of salt seemed
not to be
the statement,
hotter at the target than the surface of the sun
but the question,
what stars burn hotter at their centre?

The bird
in the frame aligned
flight
to the pressure of that
infernal cannon.

0800071, 1964

THREE SIGNS OF MORE THAN BARISTA TROUBLE

1

These daily miseries
are dirt under the grasping fingernails
that hang on to the ledge of every day
to remain between earth and the stars
for whatever lifetime you have
to grapple, roll in the dirt
of ragged bags of garden sheep manure,
maggot-lined recycle bins, torn
eco-friendly dog-shit bags. All these
are better than veterinary waiting rooms,
single-teller lunchtime bank lineups,
surprising crowds at the public library,
the plunking of robot book depositories.
And endless chains of wheeled metal
from the hermitage at the fringes,
queues on queues for our final days.

2

The radiating gravity
of these miseries,
magma one m from despair,
manifests as a kind
of never-setting, steaming concrete
flowing through a valley
pressure-washing the scrub grass,
and making ornaments of pampas deer,
nesting tapirs, termites,
and their wide and deep mounds
near freshly charred groves of jacaranda.

3

The words, the cries, locutions
apt and inept—they're like water,
plastic floating on its surface—
so many colours even the worst days
are flecked with one beautiful
but toxic unrecycled utterance—
the northern lakes tweaked green in the heat
the algae love to bloom in.
In the depths of a Pacific chasm,
a leviathan the size of a long-fallen moon
yawns a tsunami of wavelength too long
to be audible, amplitude too low
to be noticed. Not a knuckle hair stirs
when you drink the sea foam
from your vanilla latté.

ENTROPY PSALM

Unfathomable, ineffable particle
collisions, handshaking quants, who trade
degrees in markets of the infrared,
this—word, wood, ink—emerges not from will
but from the fact of turbulent exchange.
From gradients of the accidental,
never aspirational, flux, they arrange
themselves in a microscopic interval.
Oxygen, sigh of algae, grass, and tree.
Lung, mutation of the ex-marine gill.
Breath, late-blooming fuel pump of the blood. We
aspire to more than the nothing the body
will retire to, consequence of your spin
never walking back the time we're living in.

QUESTIONABLE SOCIAL MEDIA METAPHOR

Someone said the monarch butterflies
posed on milkweed pods we cultivate
to help sustain their species are the souls
of migrant children interned in camps.
Of course! They are delightfully coloured
creatures, motley fairies in ragtag
wisp-garments blotched with orange, white, and black,
whelps cooing in the desert under the moon
in seclusion, kits mewling for food
they might never have missed if not for parents
swarming here, infesting the southern border
we invest in. I don't know what scripture
prohibits a soul from early departure,
its pre-mortem 21 grams migrating to
a lighter being. You find this depressing?
Won't argue with that. But I'm not
shaking my fist in a public square.
I know Bill won't. One of his kids might—
Ashley, not Cam. Look: a hummingbird
darts between the columbine and pansies,
patriotic blooms, perfect for July!

NO SPARROW HAWKS NEARBY

Rather wake sparrowfarts in Cheshire
than intubated at dawn in leafless spring.
Welcome the sparrow that welcomes you.

Your hospital window's not dusted with frost;
weather fogs the glass sparrow-safe,
so the ounceling can hover there and sing.

Cheshire sparrows can mate with their distant
Kanata cousins, assuming tweets translate.
Their colonization of America

from a Brooklyn beachhead ca. 1850
confirms this speculation. These autonomous
flying fleur-de-lys announce more than spring.

Choirboys on budding pergolas, they chatter
in the morning to make the sky music
to their discerning mates' ears. They're our shadow

diasporas, seeding the land we settled—
never settling accounts—with generations of song.
They've fed on surplus grain we've cast away

since the barley keepers in Jericho
dropped a handful of seeds in the dust when they
poured bushels into sacrificial flames

to please the Neolithic weather gods.
If for nothing else, thank them for airborne
insect pest control, singing while they work.

And we pet their purring nemeses
whose systematic sparrowcide cuts short
millions of their melodic lives.

MAPLE SUGAR

Looking out the window at the pollinating
sugar maple's lemon-lime spattering
of flowers, buds, and infant leaves, you praise
the inherent virtue of simplicity.
Maybe you're onto something. This world
suspends such delicate blooms mid-air
on trunks and branches that carry the weight
of the crown even when we provoke the wind
to unnatural fits—gales, squalls, twisters,
nor'easters, wreckhouses toppling trains.
Roots interlace the soil though they're not deep;
most maples shrug it off with some dead twigs.
All that sap sucked from the water table
by the sun—and it transpires;
without heart or lungs, a maple breathes.
The light diet of solar spectrum, earth,
water, and a little smoke from the air
makes the robin's habitat possible,
a niche for its niche and clear sky shells.
And yet, to know the spectrum of the sun
without an ethics of its use, without
a chain of consequences understood,
we press fourteen billion thumbs on a scale
of unknown measure. The physics tells us
we accelerate imbalances.
If we wish to be conscious of the world,
we should be conscious of it as it is.
A drop of water isn't simple;
its radiolaria architects
construct sacred temples for themselves.
That worm in a puddle isn't simple,
gasping for air, pathfinding for dry curb
as you once gasped for air in a riptide
and mercifully learned to tread water.

The fresh-caught trout frying in your skillet
thrived in a pond with a thousand species.
Everything is elementary
arithmetic balanced on a ledger
until events press your life or livelihood
against the surface of unexpected
new geometries. You long for Euclid's
flat earth planes and straight lines, though the Airbus
you board to travel south flies great circles.
Go ahead, prove it with a globe and string.
You long for days of smooth particulars,
distinctions ancestors made with a glance.
The days of "Hello, Jack. Goodbye, Jane."
So long, certitude. Truth is a swarm
of flies under the tree canopy.
No matter how many you smudge between
your palms, the swarm retains its shape.
The flies enter your nostrils now. Sleep.

IF YOU WANT TO HELP, LISTEN

I walked by Phillipa's house on Springfield.
One of her paving stones was out of whack,
half on the declining path from her house,
half on the sidewalk, with an inch of air
where the angles met. Space to snap it
if a rambunctious teenager ran by
or a courier delivered a parcel.
I wandered back and sheepishly nudged
the granite tile in place with my steel toe
against coarse gravel that pushed back.
A squirrel threw an acorn down and I saw
firelight chrysanthemums in her garden,
a last rose clutching pink and coral hues
against the sub-zero pull of last night's frost.

STILL FROM DECLASSIFIED NUCLEAR TEST FILM: PROJECT PLOWSHARE

How happy the world would be
to dig a pit with light,
to sprawl the mantle
for miles
with the deeply drilled
fusion of
the heavy water spade:
to dig with
the thing a desert people
dig for.

How unhappy I would be
to dig a garden,
inedible, full of radiating colours
from so much invisible light.

Imagine these lines by
repurposed sappers,
engineers:
between my finger and thumb
the heavy water rests
snug as a gun.
I'll dig with it.

0800035, 1968 & 1973

THE SPOKESPERSON FOR THE MINISTER OF CULTURE ADDRESSES CERTAIN QUESTIONS CONCERNING THE WORKS OF STUART ROSS

Let me be ambiguous about something.
When it comes to cats on screen doors,
if I understand your analogy, Bill,
you're obviously fishing, these are subjects
over which the minister has no purview.
I can say from personal experience
a cat climbing a screen door is
a predator without prey—the swallow
outside, well, let it fly, the cat has no hope.
On the question of Stuart Ross, I believe
I have been nothing if not ambiguous,
but let me take this moment to point out
that the minister finds your insinuations
impertinent, libellous, malicious, false.
The minister could not have been more
ambiguous. This is not a yes-or-no
question of cultural policy. If you ask me,
and you did, it could be a question, I don't know,
maybe a question of the words we used.
Please let me answer with as little clarity
as possible, Bill. Our ministry has
established a policy that will lead
to the terms of reference for the study
of the landscape of that question—the hills
and valleys of the social topography
for a sensitive question of that nature.
Once that study is complete, the minister
will have established the framework to
delicately obfuscate the entire subject.
It may be true. The minister made certain
nuanced assumptions concerning the policy
and it may be that slightly more than none

of those assumptions were not precisely
rooted in evidence that might satisfy you—
but those we consulted were entirely satisfied.
To revisit the analogy you put forward,
Bill, if you carefully studied a cat
on a screen door, its fish-fed fur caressed
by August breezes intimating storms,
you might phrase your question differently.
Look—the cat on the screen door is a symbol
of exactly nothing, and I find your tone
irresponsible; it could have consequences.
To be perfectly ambiguous, a cat
has claws. It wants a surface on which to prowl.
It desires the bark of a tree to sharpen
its claws; lacking a tree in domestic space,
tattered rugs, shag carpet, a flat packed
Ikea table leg must suffice.
Bill, have you ever really looked, I mean
carefully examined with an open
and meditative eye, the alabaster
crescent sword of a cat's claw?
I impute no cultural, metaphorical,
or other meaning to the source of the table
or the specific shape of the claw referenced
in response to the question asked.
I will take one more question. Sandra.
If you'll bear with me here, let me explain
the policy of the ministry by an analogy.
There are two types of people in this world, Sandra,
those who want to take a cup of coffee
from a warm hand, and those who want the coffee
served on the table—this is true on a plane,
in a restaurant, in the morning at the office.
That's the way people are, Sandra.
It's a matter of public safety and you know it.

PSALM OF THE ENEMY

Lord, I am besieged by enemies; but,
if I am completely candid with You
and with myself, I have given them cause.
It's high time You smote me. But not my tribe;
the injustice of collective punishment
preempts divine retribution for them.
Too many mothers and children have died
from dwelling with the man who fired the shot.
Smite me, Lord, for harvesting earth's green lungs
for paper, fouling salmon streams with microbeads,
one-ton CO_2 flights to Martinique,
pension investments in Raytheon.
Send plague, earthquakes, hurricanes, and flames,
eternal winter! Only on me, Lord!

ABSOLUTE ZERO, YOU

I miss the old absolutes. I'm familiar
with the new ones. I try
to comply. But the old absolutes
carried with them a summer lake
smell at dawn when the frogs
trumpeted Reveille and the bass
fed on surface damselflies.
The old absolutes had something
of the dump about them, a dump
out of sight, behind a berm,
planted with shrubs, so far from
town you remember only once
driving there with your father
to unload ... well, you know what.
The old absolutes were said
differently. No waivers.
I miss the old absolutes as I miss
my unborn younger brother.
If he were here now, sitting across
from me in the wicker chair
petting the dog, his left hand
knitted in white canine fur,
he would say something about the
weather and my mood, and my mother
would wheel over and whack him
with her cane. But in a loving way.
Nuance, it's time for you to go.

ADVENTURE TOURISM

We had scaled the highest peak of Mount Indifference,
knees bloody, soles blistered, lungs aching for oxygen.

We gazed on the clear-running river and fertile plain
below dispersing cumuli.

We knew that villagers harvested summer crops there,
but we had never felt so empty. I sobbed.

Ariel looked down and whispered to me,
"They will abandon the valley before we reach them."

VINTNER IN SPRINGTIME

This dirt and
a drop of dew
smear my thumb,

a tear of mud
conspiring with the sun,
and worms and beetles

under my feet,
to fill this clay cup
with the fermented

blood of grapes.
Soiled human hands
make beautiful things.

STILL FROM DECLASSIFIED NUCLEAR TEST FILM: OPERATION TEAPOT (II)

Praise the mechanical camera—
its frame rate
and sensitive clarity—light
trap for heavy metals.

The bloated, luminous
man o' war
at home
in the ocean under the moon,
captured here
with its radiating poison,

vaporizing the cable guys
that steadied its
aluminum egg sac
in unsteady wind currents
of the Mohave Desert.

These guys tethered
the sac and its nuclear fuel
to the top of a tower
that would be as fluid at its base
as all the guys were steamed
by the light of that self-illuminating moon,
with its fattening tentacles.

28100, March 7, 1955

VISITATION FROM A DEAD CAT

You see out of the corner of your eye,
as you urinate at 6 a.m.,
what might be
the temporal shadow
of your cat walking on the countertop,
spine curled, hips and chest pulled
together as if to say,
"I'm sorry about all that business
with your parents.
Not their deaths so much as
their absences before they passed."
And although you're
occasionally rational,
an evidence-based policy person,
you find yourself
naked in the bathtub
sobbing like a five-year-old
beaten for talking back.
Always such sobbing
and credulous
hair-bristling, you SOB,
you ape.

MOUTH

1

I asked you about the mouth—
you said, A fish has one if the fish has lips,
worm too.

A mouth's anatomy is
cell-less—

lips have cells: the boundary
they circumscribe;

cheeks have cells, limit
mouth extent even in cod, so sweet.

What volume of water or air,
ingress, egress,
can be said there?

Buttered cod cheeks
filled, in transit,
the space my mouth makes.

2

Prepositions applying to the mouth:
in.

The glass is on your lips,
coffee in your mouth.

Beer froth on your moustache,
barley, hops,
ale in your mouth,
water in your mouth.

You said, A mouth can be
on a mouth, in a deep
tongue-swaddling kiss.

I said, Sweetheart, the lips and tongue
are on each other,
all over each other,

but the mouth—well, my tongue's in yours
and yours in mine,

exchanging breath,
time for nothing
but expletives.

3

You beg baby, Do not put
that

in your mouth, baby,
and reach to grasp
insect, dirt, worm,

afraid to let mouth
take the daily milligram dose
of its three-kilo muck allotment
prior to earth-rest.

If baby were asleep,
its as-if-underwater
vellus-haired head
facing heaven
in a crib of soft wool under
swaying dinosaur mobiles,
how less concerned would you be

with the moth above baby's mouth,
light-bound (turn it off),

the bat flying over baby's mouth
failing to find its echo
in the box-walled nursery?

4

I said, The mouth proves
all sacred spaces
empty, yet-to-be-filled
conduits for sacred as-yet-to-bes.

You said, Every word of any use
passed through a mouth
to listening or overhearing ears,

transited the mouth for the time
it takes to say
this—all words
even

methionylthreonylthreonylglutaminylarginyl...isoleucine
those ellipsis three
hours of protean parts—
forgive me, protein parts.

Now, titin, the word for those hours—a word
a chemist can live with—a
short shorthand, tenth-of-a-second

handle for that titanic alchemical unkenning,

I asked, Is that three-hour word sacred?
You instructed me, Yes:
someone took the time to say it,
Ent-chemical word.

5

I said, I refuse to believe in something
that can't be said.

You said, All of it
will be worth saying when
a fortunate insight
sloshes through the mind of some

body that has the exhibitionist
leaning to open
the lips, breathe, and

say whatever that word will be
through the sluice of the mouth.

I said, We should all
open the mouth, throw back the head
and let the uvular clapper
ring—

no sighs, no
harrumphs, no groans—

conduct your body's living choir
from the lung organ bellows.

6

There are
deplorable mouths that ache:
tongues, cheeks that suck,

teeth through which
soap on lubricated membranes
slides.

Incidental metal replacements,
identifying re-marks,

filling the cavities in the cavity of the mouth
with echoes of
extreme, execrable
depravities of speech.

I said, I mouthed off every day
when I was under twenty,
and was punched in the mouth for it,

punched with a ring in the cheek below the eye
in the face. Dented.

7

It was, for me, a synecdoche:
my father would say, Hey,
mouth!
when I'd mouth off.

I never told him to fuck
off, to his face.

Under the breath nothing; the said thing
must be clear, audible.

You said,
If mouth is a synecdoche for you,
your mouth has

no limit—the body containing it
a torus—a ring in the nose
of a bull in the social

register of gifts
snorting its last breath, so easily
shattered
without remorse.

8

In through the mouth door,
through esophagus rex,
pausing in gut
for breath,

out through the rest you know—
we climb
the chain of the body's

words, the waste
of all unsaid things, created,
consecrated, un-
made, execrable.

I'd rather speak of what you want to hear.
I desire not biological but
verbal intimacy.

Guided by the mouth,
a breath can move
a hand, touch
and lubricate
a body stalled by

so much waste
of breath.

NOCTURNE

A bat flew
over my head.
I saw its shadow
on the road.

The cat crawled
under my bed.
I heard its claws
on the slats.

A gnat landed
on the back
of my left hand.
I felt six

hairy feet
on my hairy arm.
There must have been
a proboscis.

GARRY OAK

The sharp-tailed snake under the canopy,
the Pacific great blue heron pausing in a mire,
the short-eared owl half-awake ten metres up, invisible,
the band-tailed pigeon fluttering, oak leaf in its wake,
the northern pygmy owl awake, silent, eyeing a wren,
the purple martin darting to a nest in the top branches,
the peregrine falcon scanning above the canopy,
the Lewis's woodpecker breaking bark,
the dun skipper using vetch for cover,
the Moss' elfin feeding on stonecrops,
the western bluebird and meadowlark,
the common wood-nymph pupating in the purple top grass,
the island marble unfurling its wing foliage,
the Taylor's checkerspot chomping speedwells,
the island blue pausing on a fawn lily,
the zerene fritillary, the shield-backed bug,
the robber fly doppler-zipping by your ear,
the western pondhawk orbiting,
the yellow-legged meadowhawk airlifting prey,
the taildropper slug lubricating leaf meal,
the Roosevelt elk unhinging its forelegs, tasting the air,
the Townsend's big-eared bat, asleep,
the ermine cached under the banded cord-moss,
the twisted oak moss draping an acorn,
the Pacific gopher snake gleaming in transit through the meadow—
          Geyer's onion   farewell-to-spring
          coastal wood fern   common bluecup
          Nuttall's quillwort   blue toadflax
          California-tea   white-top aster
                    poverty clover   Macrae's clover   Howell's violet
          dense-tuft hair-sedge   winged water-starwort
                              green-sheathed sedge
          foothill sedge   golden paintbrush

Victoria owl-clover   Muhlenberg's centaury
Kellogg's rush   smooth goldfields
sharp-pod peppergrass
Macoun's meadowfoam
fern-leaved desert-parsley
seaside bird's-foot trefoil   dense-flowered lupine
small-headed tarweed   dwarf sandwort
needle-leaved navarretia   rosy owl-clover
white-lip rein orchid   fragrant popcornflower
bog bird's-foot trefoil—
the slender woolly-heads puffing their tops,
the water-plantain buttercup broadcasting the sun,
the bear's-foot sanicle wilting,
the coastal Scouler's catchfly on the small-flowered tonella,
the bearded owl-clover, the Howell's triteleia,
the yellow montane violet, the California hedge-parsley,
the Garry oak and its fire-resistant bark
that leans away from untended Douglas fir,
the arthritic knuckles of the limbs and branches
high enough above the meadow to limit fire spread,
the moss on the low branches withholding rain,
watering lichen to decompose the branch
before it falls—
the raven on a branch, the mite under the raven's wing,
the twig, the caterpillar on the twig,
the leaf, the aphid on the leaf,
the ant collecting honeydew, aphid ambergris,
the bacteria in the aphid's host cells,
the yet-to-be-named micro rhizomes under the camas,
signalling with purple flowers
a forgotten abundant underground promise,
and you, snapping a selfie under the oak's shade,
your boot soles compressing living beings

that thrive in four millennia of cultivated soil,
all drink
water
from a single
blue
reflective sphere.

CLOCK

A chestnut-haired child in a white T-shirt
and pink skirt over blue jeans dawdles
behind their grandfather as they walk up
Springfield Road where the city has installed
new water mains and sewers. The road is
a catastrophe: sand for sidewalks,
gravel-covered potholes, dumpsters, open
manholes, exposed pipes, plastic taps, steel covers,
concrete, iron, and timber retaining walls.
The city is in open heart surgery.
The child disappears behind a dumpster
and returns with a dandelion clock.
They pluck a seed and cast it on the breeze.
It lands on me. I'll plant it in a lawn.

ACKNOWLEDGEMENTS

This book is part of Ottawa's thriving ecosystem of poetry conversations, readings, small press publications, and festivals. Thanks to rob mclennan—writer, publisher, extraordinary father, best man—who published some of these poems in a chapbook with above/ground press that was launched at the twenty-fifth anniversary celebration for the press. Sean Wilson and Kira Harris of the Ottawa International Writers Festival have established one of the best festivals of ideas in Canada; many of these poems were germinated by conversations with writers at these events over more than twenty years. The team at Verse Ottawa hosts poets from around the world every year; readings by Raul Zarita, Yusef Komunyakaa, Ulrika Gernes, Collette Bryce, David Groulx, and Guy Jean made me think about poetry differently. Thanks to Rod Pederson, Monty Reid, David O'Meara, David Stymeist, and the diverse board here: https://www.verseottawa.ca/about. The Tree Reading Series has been a welcome virtual gathering during the pandemic; thanks to Brandon Wint and Avonlea Fotheringham for their work sustaining it.

Several small press publishers and e-zines published early versions of these poems: rob mclennan at https://periodicityjournal.blogspot.com/, Matthew Friedman and Theresa Smalec at thetypescript.com and politicsasletters.com, George Murray at newpoetry.ca, Pearl Pirie with the Phafours chapbook *Occasionally Rational Human*, Stuart Ross at *The Week Shall Inherit the Verse.*

None of these poems would have been written without the support and companionship of Gwendolyn Guth.

I live a few hundred metres from the Ottawa River. I slept within earshot of the occupation of Ottawa by an anti-democratic, largely racist, sometimes violent convoy of small vehicles and commercial trucks, led by the white supremacist Pat King. It was difficult to live with blaring horns and aggressive harassment—one woman draped in a Canadian flag offered me earplugs with a sneer and demanded I remove my mask; a friend of mine was punched in the face twice. I wondered, does the stress and rage give me insight into the emotions an Indigenous person might feel as I walk along the Kitche Zibi (great river) at Odawa (to trade) without consequences for my largely unearned occupation of this space? It's inadequate to acknowledge that I live on unceded land. I'm reading the documentation at University of Manitoba's National Centre for Truth and Reconciliation (https://nctr.ca/) and working to commit to memory the ninety-four calls to action here: https://ehprnh2mw03.exactdn.com/wp-content/uploads/2021/01/Executive_Summary_English_Web.pdf.

Ingrid Dabringer composed the cover image for this book from Creative Commons 3.0 image "Phage.jpg" by Professor Graham Beards and the public domain image "Earth Pacific jul 30 2010.jpg" from NASA. Check out her work here: https://ingriddabringer.wordpress.com/.

Michael Dennis was one of the first poets I met when I moved to Ottawa. He was always warm, receptive, and open. His poetry is direct, honest, clear, and human. I cherish the conversations I had with him in his poetry-filled office and at his small kitchen table. For many years, he was the only poet I hand-made mock-ups of my manuscripts for. His reviews at Today's Book of Poetry (http://michaeldennis.blogspot.com/p/about_7.html) had global reach. Michael died at the end of 2020.

Peter Van Toorn, author of *Mountain Tea* (Véhicule Press, 2003) taught me most of what I know about poetry. He died in 2021. I miss his phone calls, long quotes of Hart Crane, and ludicrous jokes.

My daughter, Danica Brockwell, inspired many of the poems in this book.

NOTES

FLEE THE CELESTIAL GLITTERING OF TWILIGHT PHUKET SKYSCAPES. I've seen the bioluminescent bacteria *vibrio harvey* in the Caribbean. I have never been to Phuket, but it seemed to me the most distant, exotic location to witness a natural process that seems mystical. Trillions of these illuminated, often pathogenic bacteria use the aptly named chemical luciferase to light up the seas with increasing brightness as they thrive in warming temperatures: https://www.the-scientist.com/notebook/milky-seas-can-be-spotted-from-space-69259.

SAINT PATRICK. The poet I am thinking of is Stephen Dobyns. Here is the photograph I took when the events of the poem happened as described. You can see the crow on the lamppost at the top.

Saint Patrick is believed to have evangelized on his return to Ireland from Birdoswald, a Roman settlement at Hadrian's Wall. It's believed the gospel took so long to reach the peasants at Aspatria that Saint Patrick's ash walking stick took root. Men of my age and upbringing often reach the end of their lives before learning the limits of domination as a way of solving problems. I remain in the problem definition stage.

WHY YOU CAN'T HAVE BEAUTIFUL THINGS. Bumblebees, members of the *bombini* tribe, pollinate a wide range of native plants and commercial grain crops in North America. Bumblebees do not produce commercially viable volumes of honey, unlike their invasive foreign competitors, the overwintering honeybee, *Apis mellifera*.

STILL FROM DECLASSIFIED NUCLEAR TEST FILM. Look up these brief documentary films collected by the Lawrence Livermore National Laboratory: https://www.youtube.com/playlist?list=PLvGO_dWo8Vfc-mGi66wKRy5z-GlJ_OQND5.

Wear protective eyewear, preferably polarized goggles with UV protection. For each of these poems, I examined a single frame or brief sequence of frames out of context to resist the psychotic nihilism of these atmospheric nuclear tests, the apex of human industrial military violence.

CONVOCATION ADDRESS. Computational Politics and Cultural Calculus of Personhood are areas of significant academic research. Egyptian embalmers made no attempt to preserve the brain. The heart was the only organ they reincorporated. Corpses were excerebrated using a thin metal rod inserted in the nostril.

INCOMPLETE UNDERSTANDING OF CLOUDS. Sylvia Plath's poem "Poppies in October" haunts me.

SCHRÖDINGER PSALM. The odds of a tossed coin landing on its edge is comparatively high: one in six thousand or so.

NO SOLICITING. The voice in this poem belongs to an imaginary resident of an enormous house vastly too large for his tiny mind.

SOUTH FLORIDA VACATION is dedicated to the community of the Marjory Stoneman Douglas High School in Parkland, Florida.

PORTRAIT OF THE POET IN THREE CONCUSSIONS. The number of concussions reflected here is a lower bound estimate. It was not common practice to treat concussions in the early 1970s. My ability to recall the circumstances of these events declines annually.

SUNKEN MONUMENTS. Gutzon Borglum is the white supremacist you may not know enough about. A recently appointed Supreme Court justice who cries like Marlon Brando in his prime has a prominent jaw.

ENTROPY PSALM. I find entropy—the measure of disorder in a system—a challenging concept. The word was coined by the German physicist Rudolph Clausius in 1868 during his work on the laws of thermodynamics. The original Greek word he borrowed from suggests "a turning toward"; the universe turns toward disorder. His second law states that the entropy of a closed system always increases. The eloquent and thoughtful physicist Sean Carroll explains the relationship between entropy and time here: https://calteches.library.caltech.edu/4326/1/Time.pdf.

NO SPARROW HAWKS NEARBY. Eugene Schieffelin imported English house sparrows to the United States to control an infestation of linden moth larvae in the 1850s. Domestic cats diversify their diet by hunting these and numerous other songbirds. Sparrow populations appear to be in decline. Fluffy *Felis catus* is, however, among the planet's more destructive species: https://www.pnas.org/doi/10.1073/pnas.1602480113. This member of the number one invasive species writes editorial notes like this to feel better about his membership in the super-predator club.

MOUTH. The unfathomably enormous protein titin gives muscles elasticity. It may be that you can't speak without it, since the muscles that construct the emptiness of the mouth number about one hundred. You can find a surprisingly musical automated performance of the formal chemical name for titin on YouTube here: https://www.youtube.com/watch?v=7FoJWhHRa8s. You can have your phone read it to you before bed. Here is a companion sound poem made by adding lineation to the first few hundred characters of the 189,918-character numerologically parsimonious name.

Methionyl threonyl
threonyl glutaminyl
arginyl tyrosyl glutamyl
seryl leucyl phenyl alanyl
alanyl glutaminyl leucyl
lysyl glutamyl arginyl
lysyl glutamyl glycyl alanyl
phenylalanyl valyl

prolyl phenyl alanyl valyl
threonyl leucyl glycyl aspartyl
prolyl glycyl isoleucyl glutamyl
glutaminyl seryl leucyl
lysyl isoleucyl aspartyl threonyl leucyl
isoleucyl glutamyl alanyl glycyl alanyl
aspartyl alanyl
leucyl glutamyl leucyl glycyl
isoleucyl prolyl phenyl alanyl
seryl aspartyl prolyl leucyl alanyl

GARRY OAK. West coast Indigenous cultures cultivated Garry Oak ecosystems for thousands of years prior to contact with European settlers. Genocidal policies have ensured there are few living people with knowledge of the highly productive, multigenerational agricultural practices that fostered trade and subsistence crops of camas (*Camassia*) and acorns. The Nature Conservancy of Canada (https://www.natureconservancy.ca/en/where-we-work/british-columbia/featured-projects/salish-sea/cowichan-garry-oak-preserve.html) acquired a substantial Garry Oak preserve in the Cowichan Valley on Vancouver Island. I was given a tour of this site by Larry White accompanied by the environmental geographer Krystal Larocque. This poem would not have been possible without their generosity, knowledge, and patience.

Stephen Brockwell is a Montreal poet living in Ottawa. His sixth book, *All of Us Reticent, Here, Together* (Mansfield, 2016) won the Archibald Lampman Award for poetry. Stephen is a director of the Tree Reading Series, one of Canada's oldest poetry series, with Avonlea Fotheringham and Brandon Wint. After thirty years in IT, Stephen now works for Esri, the Environmental Systems Research Institute. Stephen has participated in the Engineering Change Lab process for transforming engineering practice toward sustainable infrastructure and communities.